The Little Book of Anxiety Fixes

The struggle between the Almond and the Seahorse

L.D. Corne

Lorraine D. Corne

Trained as a psychologist at the University of NSW, Lorraine specializes in relationships and individual counselling. She has helped individuals, couples, families and adolescents over the past 25 years.

No two people are the same, and Lorraine draws on her breadth of experience to understand the fundamental thinking behind their behaviour. Writing a book on anxiety gave Lorraine the opportunity to share the different methods she has used with her clients to help reduce one of the most pervasive afflictions in our society today.

Lorraine was both State and National Chair of the Australian Psychological Society College of Counselling Psychologists. Over the years Lorraine has been quoted in the media on numerous psychological issues, and has been a guest on the popular TV program, The Living Room.

PREFACE

I wrote The Little Book of Anxiety Fixes after seeing so many people struggle with anxiety. Most anxious people have been given very few options to deal with difficult situations.

Over 25 years in professional practice I have been to many workshops, read many books and articles, learned to master many therapies. Many of these techniques were very helpful for clients as well as myself. I wanted to share simple ways for people who lead busy lives and can't find the time to read long self-help books or attend therapy to overcome anxiety.

This book does not take the place of therapy but it does start anxious people changing the way they address difficult situations. In trying out some of these methods and realising that some may work for you, you are already making inroads into feeling better and more confident.

I am unable to remember where all of these situations originated but I will acknowledge some. The ones that have stood out for me are probably among the first self-help books I read. Please contact me if I have inadvertently used an idea that requires acknowledgment and I am only too happy to do so.

I would like to thank my two daughters for their amazing encouragement and faith in me and assistance in editing.

I would also like to thank my husband and mother for instilling in me the confidence to write.

Acknowledgements:

Albert Ellis: Rational Living
Thomas A. Harris: I'm OK, You're OK
Nathanial Branden: How to Raise Your Self-Esteem
Tom Hopkins: How to Master the Art of Selling
Antony Kidman: from Thought to Action
Manuel J. Smith: When I Say No I Feel Guilty

TABLE OF CONTENTS

Twisted thinking 3

How did your anxiety start? 6

Anxiety fix # 1: The Seahorse & the Almond...........7

Anxiety fix #2: Mind reading...................................16

Anxiety fix #3: Worry..18

Anxiety fix #4: Phobias 24

Anxiety fix #5: Humour...28

Anxiety fix #6: A barrier...30

Anxiety fix #7: Just in time.....................................31

Anxiety fix #8: OMG 32

Anxiety fix #9: The Pause 34

Anxiety fix #10: Confrontation................................36

Anxiety fix #11: Changing speech............................39

Anxiety fix #12: Being defensive 43

Anxiety fix #13: Qualities..45

Anxiety fix #14: Imagination 49

Twisted thinking

WORRY...WORRY...WORRY

Most people at some time in their lives feel overwhelmed by anxiety, worry and stress. Dealing with these sabotaging feelings for years on end can make you feel quite depressed.

Unfortunately, no fairy godmother is going to appear to take away those feelings with a wave of her wand. This book is all about having YOUR OWN wand to *EMPOWER* you to get rid of those feelings yourself. It's time to start introducing *LITTLE FIXES*, changing the way you see difficult situations and being able to REDUCE those feelings quickly.

Totally twisted thinking causes some of our most stressful thoughts.

Albert Ellis, an American psychologist, gave us a dozen of the most potent.

Do any on the list below apply to you?

☑ Tick the boxes that do.

A list of twisted thoughts

I must be approved of and loved by everyone. .... ☐

I must be perfect in everything I do. .... ☐

People reject me unless I please them. .... ☐

My value as a person depends on how much I achieve. .... ☐

Lasting relationships depend on my being unselfish. .... ☐

If people disapprove of me, it means I must be
wrong or bad. .... ☐

Being alone is the worst thing that could happen. .... ☐

My happiness depends on others. .... ☐

I must have somebody or something stronger
than myself to rely on. .... ☐

The answer to all my problems is
out there somewhere. .... ☐

OUT THERE, OUT THERE, OUT THERE SOMEWHERE...

Did you tick this list thinking,
"Well, most of that list is perfectly normal thinking.."
Yes, you are right. All those thoughts appear to be normal thinking, except for the fact that they are more likely to lead to anxiety.

The reason is that most of the thinking that leads to anxiety is from twisted, irrational thinking. So any of those boxes you have ticked, when you look at them more closely, the thoughts are quite rigid. They contain many 'musts' and 'shoulds' and 'have to's'.

Wouldn't it be great to have ideas in your head that settled you down instead of stirring you up?

That's what you are going to do by the end of this book.

Let's not waste any more time!

GET THOSE FIXES!!!

How did your anxiety start?

Any of the below apply to you?

1. Genetics
If one or both parents are anxious you will likely be anxious because:
You have a predisposition to react anxiously

And/Or

You adopt your parents' anxious reactions to non-life threatening situations just by being around them

2. Past Events
Traumatic or scary events in the past can lock inside your memory. The memories influence any situation that reminds you of the trauma. Although below your conscious level the memories can have a huge impact on your emotional responses.

3. Haven't got a clue!

Anxiety fix #1:
The Seahorse & the Almond

Anxiety can be experienced as a slight
feeling of unease to a full-blown panic
attack. The same hormones are released
when you feel excited or anxious so it is
possible to *get totally confused* about the feeling
you are experiencing.

Knowing what is happening in your body
is the first fix. It isn't scary if you know why
the feeling is there.

Let's look at the brain first and see its
influence.

Here's how the brain looks and the two essential parts involved in anxiety.

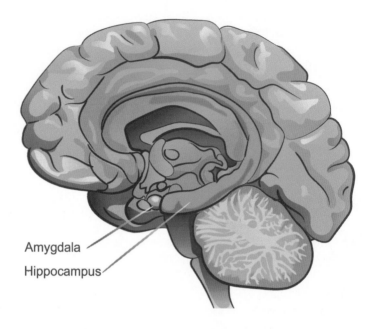

Amygdala
Hippocampus

THE KEY INFLUENTIAL PARTS are the Hippocampus and the Amygdala.

To put it simply:
The Hippocampus is responsible for new memories.

The Amygdala is responsible for old memories.

AMYGDALA

(means Almond in Greek. Look at its shape-it actually looks like an almond!)

When you think of events from long ago, the memory has been laid down in the Amgydala.
If the memory was a traumatic one you will most likely react with fight, flight or freeze.

Amygdala, being the old brain, will make you react instinctively without thought, only feeling...that's right...the OMG feeling!

The Amygdala has its place when there is a real life-threatening situation you are facing. **The rest of the time it distorts reality to look like a life-threatening situation.**

HIPPOCAMPUS

(means SeaHorse in Greek – Guess what it resembles? You got it! A seahorse!)

The Hippocampus, on the other hand, is where you lay down new memories and react to a situation rationally and maturely.

When you have an intense experience the Hippocampus (the Seahorse) shuts down due to the AMYGDALA (Almond) taking over and leaving you with the OMG feeling.

How can you switch the Hippocampus (Seahorse) back on?

The trick is to neutralise the old memory.

Neutralising the old memory

OMG – It's another social event.
GETTING READY FOR A PARTY is a
situation where you can bring on an anxiety
attack because you confuse
EXCITEMENT with ANXIETY.

And you become a
WET BLANKET
To yourself!!!!

If you have a negative experience at a social event
where you thought you made a fool of yourself,
the experience may become your default memory
for any social event in the future.

Every time you go to a party
you remember being foolish and
embarrassed.

Suddenly you are full of anxiety
each time an invitation appears.

Eventually it may be impossible to
go to a social event without panicking.

**The invitation triggers the old
memory.**

OMG it's a dog!

A dog may have jumped up and bitten
you in the past. Every time you see a
dog now you jump.
That is your old memory.

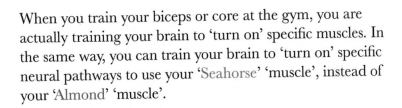

So how do you change your brain to
respond differently?

Well, the brain acts like a muscle.

When you train your biceps or core at the gym, you are
actually training your brain to 'turn on' specific muscles. In
the same way, you can train your brain to 'turn on' specific
neural pathways to use your 'Seahorse' 'muscle', instead of
your 'Almond' 'muscle'.

So...returning back to the dog scenario, a trained brain will
let you be near dogs without panicking.

You may not want to pat them, but your 'Seahorse' is
switched on and you feel in control of the situation. And,
guess what?

You won't need to panic.

Panic attacks

Let's mention an OMG occasion when you sense a sudden upsurge of anxiety you can't control.

You may feel a whole host of awful symptoms:
pounding heart   dizziness
sweating   tight chest   nausea

These feelings may be so frightening you think you are having a heart attack!!!!!

OR WORSE... experiencing some dreadful catastrophe like dying, fainting, making a fool of yourself, vomiting, or totally losing control.

Our little Almond, the Amygdala, is having a field day. Without intervention you may end up in a panic cycle whereby the fear of a situation becomes worse than the actual event.

You will be more afraid of a panic attack happening again

**Don't panic!
It's not the end of the world.**

Let's STOP the thinking that starts all this.

HERE IS THE PATTERN

When you get a THOUGHT...

It turns into a FEELING...

And you ACT on the feeling.

If you have an OMG thought, you feel, anxious, stressed and frightened. One of the ways you may deal with it is to avoid it.

Let's look at a common anxiety-provoking situation: making a speech or presentation in front of an audience.

THOUGHT: OMG I have to make a speech

FEELING: anxiety, stress, panic, fear

ACTION: freeze, avoid, withdraw
Your body responds by sweating profusely, having a dry
mouth, crying.

WHAT'S GOING ON?

What you are actually doing is looking out at the faces
looking back at you...as if each one is going to be highly
critical of you...essentially, mind-reading what everyone in the
audience is thinking.

Obviously you can't go up to people and ask them what they
think of you?

Hey! What do YOU think of ME?????

I'll let you in on a secret. The look on their face has nothing
to do with you...

**They may have just remembered they forgot to buy
toilet paper!**

Anxiety fix #2: Mind reading

What about doing something different?

Look out

 Instead of looking out and
looking back on yourself.

Your focus has to be on
them.

Not on you.

Here is an easy trick to use:

Focus on the person in front of you.

Observe their clothes, hair, jewellery, height, and any other features that catch your attention.

Once you do that you realize that you can only hold ONE thought in your head at a time.

Your mind will relax.
The mind-reading will stop.

For those who would like a visual image:

Imagine you have a MINER'S HELMET on.
It has a TORCH on the top facing out.

As you turn your head, everyone is LIT UP in front of you, but YOU stay in total darkness.

As no one can see you, you can have an opinion of everyone else there and not *worry* as to what they think of you.

Anxiety fix #3: Worry

Understanding worry

You can fall into one of two 'worry' categories:

Acute Worries and Chronic Worries.

Acute worries

Acute worries are a result of something you've heard that *triggers* a chain of negative associations. This usually happens below the level of consciousness.

By the time you become aware of acute worries, stress is overwhelming.

It leads to '*awfulising*', creating a major problem out of minor issues by dramatising the worry to absurd extremes.

You make small worries, BIG!

Chronic worries

Chronic Worries never seem far away from your thoughts. It doesn't seem to matter how busy or distracted you are. They cast clouds of gloom over everything!

Chronic worries may lead to anhedonia.

A hedonist is someone who enjoys everything.

An anhedonist doesn't find pleasure in anything.

If you can relate to either of these worries, *don't worry*

...just turn the page!

When worry strikes

The hours before dawn are the most vulnerable time for both chronic and acute worriers.

I recently read that Napoleon once remarked,
"I'm yet to meet an officer with 3 o'clock in the morning courage."

The cause is actually biological.

Your body temperature and blood sugar is LOW.

Your metabolism is SLUGGISH.

Without your internal strength, the Almond can turn on the 'RADIO CRAZY' thinking in your brain.

Worries about health, money, career, or relationships CHASE USELESSLY around your head, driving sleep further away.

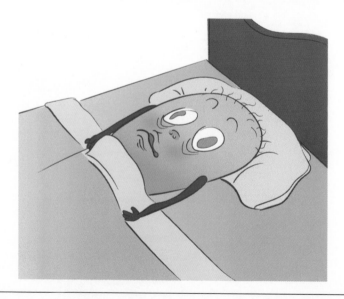

Don't stay in bed...

Use your seahorse...

Get out of bed, read a book, do a puzzle, peel some carrots, anything to get body and mind back in sync.

After half an hour go back to bed , and try again.

90% of people who do this fall asleep soon after returning to bed.

This is an effective way to switch off and snoozzzzzzze.

Worry solves absolutely nothing.

LOOK at these percentages. They are probably not totally accurate but they demonstrate a valid point...

...WHY WORRY?

40% of what we worry about never happens

30% of problems are over and done with by the time we start worrying about them

12% of worries are about non-existent health problems

10% of worries are actually focused on the wrong things

This leaves 8% of worries worth bothering about!

Someone once described to me a very funny image about worry.

Imagine your mind is only thinking
of the TERRIBLE past,
(take a step to the right).

Imagine that your mind is only thinking
of the TERRIFYING future,
(take a step to the left)

What's happening in the middle?

You just pissed on the present!

Anxiety fix #4: Phobias

Consider one particular worry and think about the worst that can happen, because that is what you dread the most but can't often voice.

For example: You may be AFRAID OF FLYING.

So you might think the worry is being trapped on the plane and no way to get out.

If you dig deeper what is the real worry?

The real worry may be EMBARRASSMENT, making a FOOL of yourself, PASSING OUT in front of other passengers, having this TERRIBLE feeling the whole 14 hour flight.

The Almond is in full flight before you even get on the plane.

Let's ask ourselves some reality check questions.

1. How likely is your worst fear to happen?
   For example: how likely is it that you will make a fool
   of yourself on the flight

   Rate this from 1 = very unlikely to
                    5 = virtually certain

2. How accurate is my information?
   For example: How many times in the past have you
   seen others embarrass themselves?

   Rate this from 1 = very doubtful to
                    5 = absolutely reliable

3. Are there practical steps you might take to prevent
   this happening?

   Rate this from 1 = many practical steps to
                    5 = can't do anything about it

4. How serious are the likely consequences of feeling
   embarrassed?

   Rate this from 1 = trivial to
                    5 = disastrous

Check out your scores:

a)   If your score was between 5 and 10, the worry is too
     trivial to waste further time on.

b)   If your score is above 16 nothing you can do seems
     likely to improve matters, so you may as well stop
     worrying.

c)   If your score is between 11 and 15, worrying would
     seem a course you could follow.
     BUT you could look at it as a CALL TO ACTION
     rather than a time to sit with despair.

(Just to give you an idea what a 16+ score looks like:

I'm afraid to die. How likely is this to happen?
5: virtually certain.

How accurate is my information?
5: because I don't know anyone who has lived forever.

Are there practical steps I might take to improve the situation?
5: I'm going to die whatever I do.

How serious are the likely consequences?
At least a 4!

That makes a score of 19 so if I keep worrying about dying I make every
day of my life sad instead of embracing it. Dying is too inevitable to keep
worrying about it.)

Taking action

Taking action helps channel all that adrenalin (produced by the glands that the Almond is stimulating) into an achievement.

The Seahorse therefore can take over and return calm and focus.

If your Seahorse is working you can:

a)   Take practical steps to improve the situation

b)   Find out more about what is happening

c)   Develop a plan for avoiding or lessening the consequences of what is happening

d)   Put your worries into perspective

If your Seahorse is still sinking and not swimming... move to anxiety fix #5.

Anxiety fix #5: Humour

HUMOUR will conquer anxiety.

Develop an image that focuses on a
WILDLY ABSURD SCENARIO

Remember the plane scenario where you are
afraid of having a panic attack on the plane?
(That fear is the pesky Almond at work!)

Now imagine that every passenger on the plane decides to
have a panic attack. Everyone is rolling around in the aisles,
trays going everywhere. Each person's Almond is totally out
of control.

If it makes you giggle...
the Seahorse IS BACK IN CONTROL

Have you ever been stressed due to a delay in traffic, or had a client upset with your work? Chances are that you have started to think of the consequences in their worst-case scenario

- Oh no! I'm going to be criticised!
- I'll be fired! (That's one frantic Almond)

Using an absurd image will bring back the Seahorse and introduce humour and perspective to the situation, as in the example below.

You have just walked through the door late. Your client sees you and is SO furious they attack you with a huge carving knife, angry froth foaming at their mouth, eyes bulging from their sockets. Imagine them pulling a trapdoor that drops you into a bottomless pit as they cry,

"Perish all who arrive late for a meeting."
The more vivid and ridiculous you make this exaggeration, the **greater its power** to reduce stress.

Your worries seem **absurd** rather than threatening.

Anxiety fix #6: A barrier

Create a mental barrier to worry

You are sitting at work and a worrying thought comes into your head.

Think immediately "yellow unicorns", picturing them as vividly as possible, flying around the room right now. Remember you can only hold one thought in conscious awareness at a time! If you focus on a totally different topic this will create a barrier to worry.

Now try the old switcheroo trick! Switch your attention to some task that is enjoyable and requires concentration.

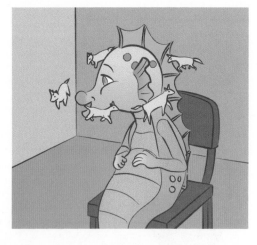

Otherwise start thinking of something enjoyable you are going to do later. The worrying thought (the annoying Almond), will disappear and be replaced by the Seahorse.

The task at hand becomes the priority and the world around you maintains its perspective. Yeah!

Anxiety fix #7: Just in time

'Just in time' worry

You may have to sit exams or attend an interview. You lie wide awake in the night, churning the situation over in your mind.

The Almond is having a great time pumping up your adrenalin. Your thoughts alight on failure and humiliation, as well as letting yourself down and everyone else.

I'LL WORRY AT 9 AM TOMORROW

When worry involves something some time in the future, use **"Just in Time Worry"**. Tell yourself, I have a right to be concerned but since *nothing bad* is going to happen until tomorrow morning, that's when I will start worrying,

WORRY achieves nothing but tiredness and distractions. Worry only when you are actually there... and then discover there was nothing to worry about!

The Seahorse has taken back control.

Any time you are worried return to the 4 reality check questions on page 25 and give yourself a reality check to see if your worry is worth worrying about. If it is, try and conquer it with the fixes you have just learned.

Anxiety fix #8: OMG

Remember when we looked at OMG Thought, Feeling and Action? Here is another strategy to change your anxiety level.

OMG (thought+feeling+action)= paralysis

OMG THOUGHT:
I was thinking of all the things I want to get done over the weekend.

OMG EMOTION = ANXIETY
(The Almond is doing its thing)

Let's stop for a moment and think through what kind of OMG thought you can have that turns ordinary tasks into mountains of anxiety.

OMG THOUGHT:
I was thinking of all the things I want to get done over the weekend.

OMG EMOTION:
I'M ANXIOUS (Almond doing its thing)
The automatic thought that came before the feeling went like this:

OMG AUTOMATIC THOUGHT:
I'll never get all of this done. It's too much for me.

**However: anxious anecdotes can turn into calm
seahorses when you use the following thinking.**

Rational response:
(Seahorse doing its thing)
I've done more than this before and there is no law that says I
have to get it all done.

What just happened?

I don't feel convinced by the automatic thought.
I can now look at the task more systematically, perhaps even
divide it up so that the whole lot doesn't have to be done
today.

In this case, the Seahorse won the battle.

Let's try what you have learned.
    * Reduce the "awfulising"
    * Look OUT. Don't look back on yourself with
      imaginary criticisms.
    * Put on your pretend miner's helmet.

Seahorse arrives and brings perspective back to the situation.

Anxiety fix #9: The pause

Managing the stress that comes with anxiety

We all walk around with an internal level of stress. When we are children this internal level is generally very small. As we have life experiences our internal level of stress increases.

If you have many difficult times in your life the stress may overwhelm you.

That's when you reach for extra help via doctors prescribing medication, alcohol or recreational drugs, or just soldier on.

For a while these help mask how you feel but, when they wear off, your internal level of stress returns to the same high level. You are once again feeling overwhelmed.

Let's manage stress better by using stress management.

Remember what happens when you get stressed?

Your Almond is pumping the adrenalin around your body to prevent the Seahorse from even getting a look-in

The Seahorse influence:

When you are relaxed the muscles are long and smooth, the blood flow increases around the body and flows into the brain. You no longer think automatically because you are able to PAUSE.

The pause:

When you are able to PAUSE you can consider what the other person has said, and look at the situation with different eyes...

not just with the ALMOND'S perspective...
You can't help but feel anxious, unsafe, immature

But with the SEAHORSE'S Mature perspective:
You will feel focused, confident, in control...

You can use many different types of stress management.

Once you are able to use the PAUSE, you can begin to use effective techniques when faced with difficult people or situations.

You are able to bring your rational Seahorse back in charge.

CHAPTER 12
Anxiety fix #10: Confrontation

Dealing with confrontation

Feeling accused is a situation that can stimulate the Almond.

You may not know the words to combat the accusations so you go into automatic defensive mode. This increases the risk of the situation either turning into an argument or having to give in and be resentful.

When you are able to PAUSE you can bring in new techniques that get rid of the Almond's influence.

Reducing the stress in your body makes it far easier to pause and not speak straight away. Then you have time to put into practice the new strategies and techniques.

Pausing can help you use your imagination.
Once you can pause use this new strategy.

Here's the fix...

Imagine the words coming out of the other person's mouth like little arrows from a cartoon character. Imagine those arrows falling into a bottomless pit that sits between you and them.

If the words are too intense imagine that you have pressed a button and an invisible glass wall rises up in front of you and the arrows hit the wall and fall back into the pit.

You feel safe.
The words are not penetrating you.
You can now decide how to respond.

This ability to 'step back' in your head allows the pause to help you detach.

The Seahorse comes back and you can say something to calm the situation.

How to respond to criticism (perceived or otherwise)

Now you are nice and relaxed and ready to receive any curve balls that come your way. Here are a few ways to deflect criticisms.

Steven Covey once said,
**"Most people do not listen with the intent to understand.
They listen with the intention to reply."**

This quote leads to...

CHAPTER 13
Anxiety fix #11: Changing speech

Active listening

Active listening is an assertive skill to combat confrontation or manipulation from the other side. When your Almond is at work, these are the types of unhelpful responses it gives.

Your partner says, "You don't understand me!"

Now if you are anxious you may fight back by saying: "Well, you don't understand me!"

Or you may use the freeze option by thinking: "What have I said now?"

Or you may use the flight/defensive option by saying, "I didn't mean to upset you."

The Almond is having another field day as its best work produces feelings of fight, flight or freeze!

Now being defensive is a very common coping strategy for anxious people. Here is a technique to help you NOT become defensive in the face of criticism, manipulation or emotional blackmail.

Let's look at an example that is a very common confrontational statement people may use to manipulate you.

1. Clarifying example

Partner says: "You don't understand me!"

1. CLARIFY

"ARE YOU SAYING I DON'T UNDERSTAND YOU?"
(Using their exact words)

The answer can be,
"Yes, that's right. You never understand me!"

Often people exaggerate their accusations.
So you need to check out that belief.

2. Checking their belief

"DO YOU REALLY BELIEVE THAT I NEVER UNDERSTAND YOU?" *(Using their exact words)*

This question allows the other side to check for themselves whether they mean a "forever" statement.

You can go back and forth with these questions until it is time to make a balancing statement.

3. Balancing statement

"SOMETIMES I UNDERSTAND YOU AND SOMETIMES I DON'T". *(These words reflect reality)*

It isn't true that someone is the same all of the time. You would be a robot rather than a human.

When you use this technique it brings the conversation back in your control.

You begin to realize that people make statements that they may not necessarily believe.

It gives you time to detach emotionally from what they are saying and decide whether they speak the truth, a lie or somewhere in-between.

The result is:

* They know you have heard them.
* Your anxiety is reduced.
* You no longer feel criticized.
* You are able to understand clearly what the other person is saying to you.
* You feel more in control as you have avoided an argument.

However, you may need a little more help in the imagination department to protect you even more.

This brings us to Anxiety Fix #12.

ANXIETY FIX #12:
Being defensive

Using an image of a table tennis table

When you become defensive it is as if you are standing at one end of the table tennis table, the balls are coming at you and you are catching them instead of hitting them back.

When you use these new verbal techniques you can imagine sending those balls back. It doesn't matter how hard the balls are coming back at you. In your head you calmly hit them back to the other side.

As described in Active Listening the first ball to send back is the clarification one. The first verbal reaction is to CLARIFY what they just said, using their EXACT WORDS.

The reason you must use their exact words is that you may misinterpret what they are saying. This cannot happen when you use this technique. Try it out keeping the image of the table tennis table in the forefront of your mind.

ANXIETY FIX #13: Qualities

Your personal qualities

I will make a bet that you haven't thought about
your own personal qualities for some time.
If you are anxious and stressed you mainly
concentrate on the other person's expectations
and generally find that you do not live up to
them.

Make a list of your own personal qualities and make sure
they are put somewhere you can read them every day.

Here is a list of examples that may apply to you:

Choose the most appropriate for yourself
and place a tick in the box.

You may like to cut this list out and place it where you can
read it.

Remind yourself of your good qualities EVERY DAY.

My qualities

I work well with others .... ☐

I am unique .... ☐

I am a warm person .... ☐

I am responsible .... ☐

I am serious .... ☐

I make good choices .... ☐

I am cooperative .... ☐

I get things done .... ☐

I include others .... ☐

I am fair .... ☐

I 'have a go' .... ☐

I am a great sport .... ☐

I am honest .... ☐

I am talented .... ☐

I have good ideas .... ☐

I am a keen worker .... ☐

I make good decisions .... ☐

I am sensible .... ☐

I am helpful .... ☐

I am lively .... ☐

I am a good friend .... ☐

I am a thinker .... ☐

I am strong .... ☐

I am peaceful .... ☐

I care .... ☐

I am determined .... ☐

I am generous .... ☐

I am cheerful .... ☐

I am a quiet person .... ☐

I am thoughtful .... ☐

I am fun to be with .... ☐

I am a smiley person .... ☐

I am generally an optimistic and happy person .... ☐

I make other people happy .... ☐

I make other people feel comfortable .... ☐

I have a great sense of humour .... ☐

I listen to what others say .... ☐

I am a good problem solver .... ☐

I am able to stand alone .... ☐

The more often you read about your good qualities the easier it is to adjust to difficult situations around you.

You are now more aware that the situation **isn't about you.**

It is about an **issue** that is **not personal**.

This is a way to stop mixing up your 'personal you' with outside issues.

You are a person with **good qualities** no matter the mess of the situation you find yourself in.

ANXIETY FIX #14:
Imagination

Using your imagination

When someone is having a go at you it is
useful to have an image that detaches you
from taking it personally.

Imagine that the person giving you an
anxious moment looks like a whirlwind.
The whirlwind is sending out lots of 'crap'
wherever it goes and you are spending your
time ducking it.

This image makes it clearer that it isn't your 'personal self'
causing this...

It is the other person's PERSONAL PROBLEMS.

Once it is clear that the negative emotion coming towards you is only the other person's almond having a field day, you can bring out your seahorse with rational pride!

Reminding yourself of the PAUSE,
to ACTIVELY LISTEN,
to DESCRIBE what they look like,
put on the MINER'S HELMET
and remembering your QUALITIES
will achieve a good result for your self-worth.

Anxiety reduced.

The struggle is over.

Seahorse
has conquered
Almond

Congratulations!

Printed in Great Britain
by Amazon

82397236R00033